LAP

WITHDRAWN

D1172037

U.S. Landforms

DANA MEACHEN RAU

Children's Press®
An Imprint of Scholastic Inc.
New York   Toronto   London   Auckland   Sydney
Mexico City   New Delhi   Hong Kong
Danbury, Connecticut

Front cover, center: Delicate Arch in Arches National Park, Utah
Front cover, top right: Niagara Falls in Niagara Falls, New York
Front cover, bottom left: Devils Tower in Wyoming

Content Consultant
James Wolfinger, PhD
Associate Professor
DePaul University
Chicago, Illinois

Library of Congress Cataloging-in-Publication Data

Rau, Dana Meachen, 1971–
  U.S. Landforms/by Dana Meachen Rau.
    p. cm.—(A true book)
  Includes bibliographical references and index.
  ISBN-13: 978-0-531-24854-6 (lib. bdg.)   ISBN-10: 0-531-24854-2 (lib. bdg.)
  ISBN-13: 978-0-531-28329-5 (pbk.)   ISBN-10: 0-531-28329-1 (pbk.)
  1. Landforms—United States—Juvenile literature. I. Title.
  GB400.6.R38 2012
  551.300973—dc23
                                                  2011031744

All rights reserved. Published in 2012 by Children's Press, an imprint of Scholastic Inc.
Printed in China 62
SCHOLASTIC, CHILDREN'S PRESS, A TRUE BOOK, and associated logos are trademarks and/or registered trademarks of Scholastic Inc.
1 2 3 4 5 6 7 8 9 10 R 21 20 19 18 17 16 15 14 13 12

Find the Truth!

Everything you are about to read is true *except* for one of the sentences on this page.

Which one is **TRUE**?

T or F The Hawaiian Islands were formed by volcanoes.

T or F All rivers in the United States flow toward the Atlantic Ocean.

Find the answers in this book.

Contents

THE **BIG** TRUTH!

NATIONAL PARK SERVICE

Many landforms are shaped by moving water.

4 The Power of Water

5 Changes Over Time

This sandstone was shaped by wind over millions of years.

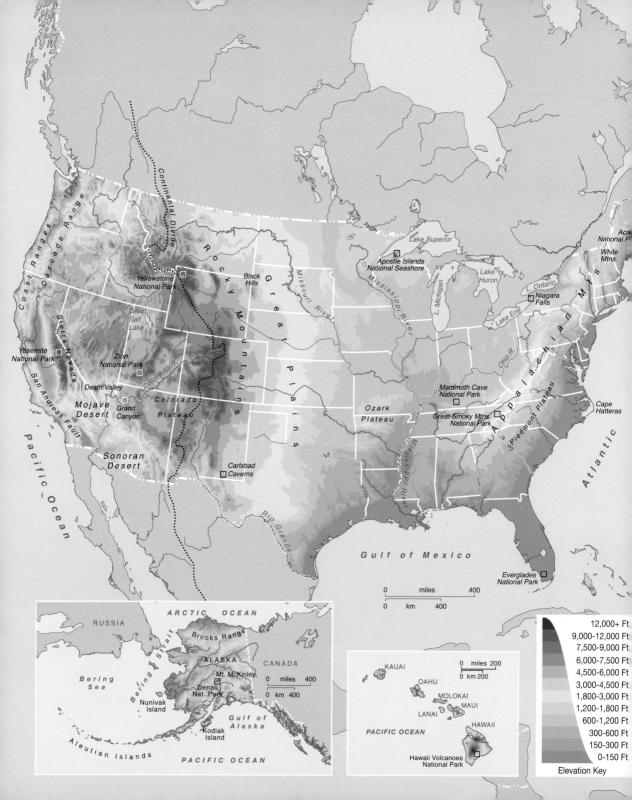

Continental Divide

Coast Ranges

Cascade Range

Rocky Mountains

Great Plains

Lake Superior

Apostle Islands
National Seashore

Missouri River

Mississippi River

Lake
Huron

Lake Michigan

L. Ontario

Niagara
Falls

Lake Erie

Aca
National P

White
Mts.

Mts.

Appalachian Mts.

Yellowstone
National Park

Black
Hills

Great
Salt
Lake

Sierra Nevada

Yosemite
National Park

San Andreas Fault

Zion
National Park

Death Valley

Colorado R.

Mojave
Desert

Grand
Canyon

Colorado
Plateau

Sonoran
Desert

Ozark
Plateau

Mammoth Cave
National Park

Great Smoky Mtns.
National Park

Ohio R.

Piedmont Plateau

Cape
Hatteras

Carlsbad
Caverns

Mississippi River

Rio Grande

Gulf of Mexico

Everglades
National Park

Pacific
Ocean

Atlantic

Scale:
0 miles 400
0 km 400

Alaska inset

ARCTIC OCEAN

RUSSIA

Brooks Range

ALASKA

CANADA

Bering Strait

Mt. McKinley

Denali
Nat. Park

Bering
Sea

0 miles 400
0 km 400

Nunivak
Island

Kodiak
Island

Gulf of
Alaska

Aleutian Islands

PACIFIC OCEAN

Hawaii inset

KAUAI

OAHU

0 miles 200
0 km 200

MOLOKAI

LANAI

MAUI

HAWAII

PACIFIC OCEAN

Hawaii Volcanoes
National Park

Elevation Key	
	12,000+ Ft
	9,000-12,000 Ft
	7,500-9,000 Ft
	6,000-7,500 Ft
	4,500-6,000 Ft
	3,000-4,500 Ft
	1,800-3,000 Ft
	1,200-1,800 Ft
	600-1,200 Ft
	300-600 Ft
	150-300 Ft
	0-150 Ft

CHAPTER 1

Take a Tour

You may know a lot about the land where you live. Maybe you drive past a forest or ride your bike up a hill. You might play in a grassy field or climb on rocks. You might have noticed the natural landforms around you, even if they are covered with roads, buildings, and other structures.

The United States has highlands, lowlands, and all types of land in between. If you took a tour across the country, you would see lots of landforms.

Borderlines

The United States is just one of the countries on the continent of North America. Canada lies to the north. Mexico lies to the south. The other borders of the United States are along coastlines. The Atlantic Ocean lies to the east and the Pacific Ocean to the west.

The Rio Grande River starts in Colorado.

The Rio Grande forms part of the border between the United States and Mexico.

This satellite image shows all five Great Lakes.

Lake Superior

Lake Huron

Lake Ontario

Lake Michigan

Lake Erie

Peninsulas

Land extends into bodies of water to form **peninsulas**. Florida is a peninsula that reaches into the Atlantic Ocean. It creates a sheltered area of ocean called the Gulf of Mexico.

Michigan has two peninsulas that reach into the Great Lakes. The five Great Lakes on the U.S.-Canadian border are the largest group of freshwater lakes on Earth.

 Rocky Mountain National Park is the highest park in the United States.

Mountains

Mountains are hard to miss! They rise high above the surrounding land. The United States has some large mountain ranges. A mountain range is a group of mountains. The Rocky Mountains stretch 3,300 miles (5,300 kilometers), starting in Alaska, running through Canada, and making their way as far south as New Mexico.

In the eastern United States, the Appalachian Mountains are much lower in **elevation**. They are also not as long as the Rockies. They stretch from Canada down to Alabama for about 1,500 miles (2,400 km).

The Coast Ranges run down the Pacific Coast from Alaska all the way into California. The Sierra Nevada and the Cascade Range are other ranges near the Pacific.

The forests of the Appalachians turn bright colors in the fall.

Plateaus and Plains

Plateaus are generally large, flat areas of land that rise sharply above the surrounding area. They cover much of the western United States. The Colorado Plateau is a large area that expands into Utah, Colorado, Arizona, and New Mexico. The Ozark Plateau makes up part of the landscape of Missouri and Arkansas.

Parts of the high Colorado Plateau have eroded over many years to create unique landforms.

This sandstone feature on the Colorado Plateau is called the Wave.

The Great Plains are home to many plants and animals.

The Great Plains sit in the middle of the country between the Rockies and the Appalachians. Plains are large, flat areas that are not as high as plateaus. The Great Plains are covered mostly with grasslands.

On the eastern and southeastern edges of the United States is the coastal plain. This area of low land stretches inland from the shoreline of the Atlantic Ocean and the Gulf of Mexico.

The San Juan Mountains in Colorado are part of the Rocky Mountains.

Making Mountains

Landforms look solid. They don't seem to move. But the earth and its land are constantly changing. The top, rocky layer of the continents and the ocean floor are called Earth's crust. This crust is made up of separate pieces called plates. Some of these plates move apart from each other, and others move closer together. Sometimes they slam into each other.

 Mount Sneffels is named after a mountain in Jules Verne's *Journey to the Center of the Earth*.

Back in Time

If you were around millions of years ago, you might have seen how the country's mountains were made. Most of North America sits on the North Atlantic Plate. Scientists believe that the Appalachian Mountains started forming more than 270 million years ago. The North American Plate crashed into the African Plate. The edges of the plates pushed upward to form the Appalachian Mountains.

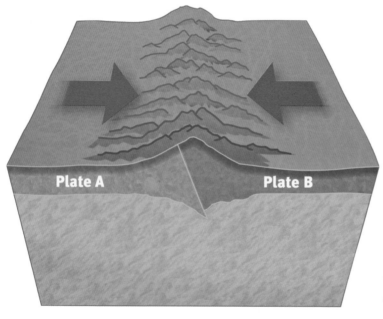

Plate A   Plate B

The edges of plates sometimes push upward when they press into each other.

Mountains also form when plates pull apart from each other. This makes large blocks of rock break into big chunks. Some of these chunks tilt upward. Others move down. The Sierra Nevada formed this way.

When two plates come together, one plate sometimes goes under the other. Scientists believe that the Pacific Plate pushed under the North American Plate, creating the Rocky Mountains.

The San Andreas Fault is easily visible on Earth's surface.

Shaking the Earth

A fault is a crack where two pieces of the earth's crust move against each other. The San Andreas Fault enters California near Santa Rosa. It travels down through the edge of the state almost to the Mexican border. The fault is on the boundary of the North American and Pacific Plates. Pressure along this fault sometimes causes earthquakes. The land trembles and shakes, causing a lot of damage.

Highs and Lows

Elevation is how high a landform is compared to the average level of the land at **sea level**.

Mt. McKinley in Alaska has the highest elevation in the United States. It stands 20,320 feet (6,194 meters) above sea level.

Death Valley (below) in California has the lowest elevation. It is 282 feet (86 m) below sea level.

Volcanoes

Mountains are also made by volcanoes. Deep underground, rock is so hot that it becomes liquid. This **molten** rock sometimes comes out of cracks in the crust as a volcano. When molten rock reaches the surface, it is called lava. This lava hardens and becomes rock. Mountains form when lava cools and hardens around a volcano.

Mount St. Helens' 1980 eruption caused destruction to much of the surrounding land.

20

Hot lava runs like a river from an active volcano in Hawaii.

Volcanoes are most common along the boundaries of plates. The area around the Pacific Ocean that gets the most volcanoes is called the Ring of Fire. The Cascade Range of California, Oregon, and Washington and the Aleutian Islands of Alaska sit along this ring. They were formed by volcanoes.

Volcanoes also erupt in the middle of plates in areas called hot spots. A hot spot in the middle of the Pacific Plate formed the Hawaiian Islands.

Glaciers moving through the area carved out the mountains and valleys of Glacier National Park.

CHAPTER 3

Carving Out Rock

During the last ice age, more than half the continent of North America was covered with **glaciers**. Glaciers are large areas of slow-moving ice. The last ice age ended nearly 12,000 years ago. But there are still glaciers at Glacier National Park in Montana and other places in the United States. Even if you don't visit a glacier, you can see how glaciers have shaped the land.

Over time, many of Glacier National Park's glaciers have melted.

Pieces of a glacier can break off and float away when the glacier moves into a body of water.

Two Types of Glaciers

Glaciers are made from layers of snow piled on top of each other. A valley glacier forms in mountain areas where the temperature is cold and snow doesn't melt away. The layers get packed down and become ice. The glacier gets heavy and starts to flow down the mountain very slowly. A continental glacier forms in flatter areas. It does not flow like a river. Instead, it spreads out into a flat sheet.

The Land Left Behind

A glacier moving down a mountain picks up rocks along the way. It moves like a conveyor belt in a factory. The heavy ice scrapes the land underneath, carving out a U-shaped valley with steep cliffs. You can see valleys like these in Yosemite National Park in California.

Yosemite lies in the Sierra Nevada.

Winters are cold and snowy at Yosemite National Park.

A large glacier sheet levels out the land beneath it. The glacier carries rocks along with it. When the glacier melts, it leaves these rocks in a new place. Moraines are mounds of rock and soil left by a melting glacier. The fertile plains of Ohio are moraines. Glaciers also leave behind large boulders that don't match the surrounding rocks in an area.

Glaciers leave lakes behind, too. As large glaciers of the last ice age melted, pieces broke off and got stuck in the ground.

Landform Timeline

About 270 million years ago
Appalachian Mountains formed.

About 70 million years ago
Rocky Mountains formed.

When a piece melted, it filled its hole with water to form a small lake called a kettle lake. Glaciers also create big lakes. The Great Lakes were carved by glaciers.

A **cirque** may form in the mountains at the head of a glacier. Cirques have a bowl shape. Tuckerman Ravine is a cirque on Mount Washington in the White Mountains of New Hampshire. Adventurous people ski down its steep slope.

About 12,000 years ago
Niagara Falls formed; the last ice age ended.

About 6 million years ago
Colorado River began carving the Grand Canyon.

About 4 to 6 million years ago
Carlsbad Caverns formed.

Protecting Natural Treasures

The government creates national parks to help protect the land, plants, and animals of an area.

YELLOWSTONE NATIONAL PARK in Idaho, Montana, and Wyoming is the world's oldest national park. It opened in 1872. Geysers of hot water shoot up from the ground.

BIG BEND NATIONAL PARK in Texas includes three very different regions to explore, including mountain, desert, and river environments.

MAMMOTH CAVE NATIONAL PARK in Kentucky preserves the world's longest system of caves.

APOSTLE ISLANDS NATIONAL LAKESHORE in Wisconsin consists of 22 islands in Lake Superior with spectacular sandstone cliffs carved during the last ice age.

ACADIA NATIONAL PARK (background photo) in Maine contains tall mountains and low coastline all in one park.

Many towns and
farms are built along
the banks of the
Connecticut River.

CHAPTER 4

The Power of Water

The frozen water of glaciers is heavy and strong enough to carve out rocks. Liquid water is powerful, too. As water runs over the land, it **erodes** the surface. Most rivers start in mountains, fed by the water of melting snow. Rivers wind back and forth, finding pathways around or across landforms. They carve out the edges of riverbanks. Water sculpts the land into different shapes.

 Rivers curve and bend with the shape of the land.

The Missouri River is a tributary of the Mississippi River.

Carried by the Flow

Water falls to the ground when it rains. The rain flows into streams. Streams join rivers. Smaller rivers, called **tributaries**, join larger rivers. Most rivers then flow until they reach a larger body of water, such as a lake or an ocean. The area that a river draws its water from is called a watershed. The largest watershed in the United States is the area drained by the Mississippi River.

As the river flows, it wears away the land and picks up rock and soil. When a river reaches a larger body of water, it slows down. It widens and drops this **sediment**. This creates a river **delta**. The Mississippi delta covers a 13,000-square-mile (33,700 square km) area where the Mississippi River enters the Gulf of Mexico.

Many ships travel through the Mississippi River delta as they make their way from the Gulf of Mexico into the United States.

Falling Water

Rivers flow from higher to lower land in the mountains or edges of plateaus. Waterfalls occur when there is a sudden drop in elevation. In the eastern United States, rivers of the Piedmont Plateau drop down to the Atlantic coastal plain. This area is home to a lot of waterfalls.

Kauai Wailua Falls in Hawaii is about 80 feet (24.4 m) in height.

34

Many pieces of broken rock lie at the base of Niagara Falls.

The Horseshoe Falls and American Falls (together called Niagara Falls) are powerful waterfalls on the Niagara River. They straddle the border between the United States and Canada. As the water flows over the steep cliffs, it erodes the rock below. Large pieces of rock break off. The falls move back a little every year as they wear away the edge. This is another example of how landforms are always changing.

People travel from around the world to see the Grand Canyon.

Creating Canyons

The Colorado River flows across the Colorado Plateau in the western United States. Over millions of years, it has carved out one of the most awesome canyons in the world. The Grand Canyon extends for 277 miles (446 km). The river has eroded the plateau up to 1 mile (1.6 km) deep in some places. Visitors can see the striped layers of the plateau's rock on the canyon's steep sides.

The Dividing Line

In the high areas of the Rocky Mountains, you'll find the Continental Divide. Rivers east of this line flow toward the Atlantic Ocean and the Gulf of Mexico. Rivers on the west side of this line flow toward the Pacific Ocean. This line is also called the Great Divide.

CONTINENTAL
DIVIDE
ELEVATION 8391

NATIONAL
PARK
SERVICE

Sand is very light
and easy for wind
to blow around.

CHAPTER 5

Changes Over Time

The same wind that pushes a sailboat helps shape the land, too. Sand covers many beaches of the coastal plain. Wind blowing inland from the ocean pushes sand into big piles called dunes. Dunes don't stay in one place. Tourists in Cape Cod may notice that the landscape of the beach changes with each visit. Dunes move slowly in the direction of the wind.

Sand dunes can help protect property from damaging storm waves.

Breaking Into Bits

Weathering is the natural process of wind, water, and other forces breaking down rocks into smaller pieces. Wind picks up sand and rubs it against larger pieces of rock. Ice gets into cracks and makes pieces of rock fall off. An earthquake shaking the ground might cause a huge piece of rock to break off a mountain. These rocks weather even more. They get smaller and smaller. Eventually, they become sand or soil.

Farmers need healthy soil to grow their crops.

Georgia's clay is red because it contains iron.

Parts of Georgia are known for their red clay, a type of soil. It even colors the dirt roads that cross through rural areas.

The color and type of soil depends on what type of rock broke down. In northeastern forests, the soil might be brown. In the prairie, it is thick, dark, and rich. In the deserts of the Southwest, it looks red.

Weathering can create unique rock formations as it breaks down rocks. Arizona's Vermilion Cliffs are an example. The natural arches in Utah are another example.

The Carlsbad Caverns are known for the amazing rock formations that hang from their ceilings and rise from their floors.

Hidden Treasures

Underground water can weather rocks, too. Chemicals in the water break down limestone. The limestone wears away and leaves caves behind. Carlsbad Caverns is an amazing network of caves hidden under the desert of New Mexico.

Change happens very slowly, sometimes over millions of years. Look up at the mighty mountains on the horizon, or down to the pebbles at your feet. They are both part of the never-ending process of changing landforms. ★

Length of the Appalachian Mountains: 1,500 mi. (2,400 km)

Length of the Rocky Mountains: 3,300 mi. (5,300 km)

Highest point in the United States: Mount McKinley (Alaska), 20,320 ft. (6,194 m) above sea level

Lowest point in the United States: Death Valley (California), 282 ft. (86 m) below sea level

Size of the Mississippi delta: 13,000 sq. mi. (33,700 sq km)

Length of the Grand Canyon: 277 mi. (446 km)

Did you find the truth?

T The Hawaiian Islands were formed by volcanoes.

F All rivers in the United States flow toward the Atlantic Ocean.

Resources

Books

Augustin, Byron. *The Grand Canyon*. New York: Marshall Cavendish Benchmark, 2010.

Gilpin, Daniel. *The Colorado River*. Milwaukee, WI: Gareth Stevens Publishing, 2004.

Jackson, Tom. *The Columbia River*. Milwaukee, WI: Gareth Stevens Publishing, 2004.

Johnson, Robin. *The Mississippi: America's Mighty River*. New York: Crabtree Publishing, Co., 2009.

Kummer, Patricia K. *The Great Lakes*. New York: Marshall Cavendish Benchmark, 2009.

Maynard, Charles W. *The Appalachians*. New York: PowerKids Press, 2004.

McNeese, Tim. *The Missouri River*. Philadelphia: Chelsea House Publishers, 2004.

Miller, Millie, and Cyndi Nelson. *The United States of America: A State-by-State Guide*. New York: Scholastic Reference, 2006.

Rau, Dana Meachen. *North America*. Chanhassen, MN: The Child's World, 2004.

Somervill, Barbara A. *The Rugged Rockies*. Chanhassen, MN: The Child's World, 2005.

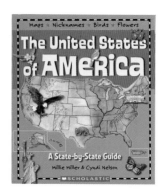

Web Sites

National Park Service

www.nps.gov/index.htm

Discover the stories, features, and wildlife of the parks at this main site of the National Park Service.

World Atlas

www.worldatlas.com/webimage/countrys/namerica/usstates/usland.htm

Find fast facts about the United States and descriptions of its many different landforms at this site.

Places to Visit

American Museum of Natural History

Central Park West at 79th Street New York, NY 10024

(212) 769-5100

www.amnh.org

View exhibits and collections that trace the natural history of the world's land, animals, and people.

Rocky Mountain National Park

1000 Highway 36 Estes Park, CO 80517

(970) 586-1206

www.nps.gov/romo/index.htm

Explore the natural beauty of the United States' largest mountain range.

Visit this Scholastic web site for more information on U.S. landforms:

www.factsfornow.scholastic.com

Important Words

cirque (SURK) — a bowl-shaped landform at the head of a glacier

delta (DEL-tuh) — the flat area at the mouth of a river where it flows into a larger body of water

elevation (el-uh-VAY-shuhn) — the height above sea level

erodes (i-ROHDZ) — wears away

glaciers (GLAY-shurz) — large areas of slow-moving ice

molten (MOHL-tuhn) — liquid because of extreme heat

peninsulas (puh-NIN-suh-luhz) — strips of land surrounded by water on three sides

sea level (SEE LEV-uhl) —the average level of the ocean's surface, used as a starting point from which to measure the height or depth of a place

sediment (SED-uh-muhnt) — material deposited by water, wind, or glaciers

tributaries (TRIB-yuh-ter-eez) — streams or small rivers that flow into larger rivers

weathering (WETH-er-ing) — the process of breaking rocks into smaller pieces

Index

Page numbers in **bold** indicate illustrations

About the Author

Dana Meachen Rau is the author of more than 300 books for children. A graduate of Trinity College in Hartford, Connecticut, she has written fiction and nonfiction titles including early readers and books on science, history, cooking, and many other topics that interest her. She especially loves to write books that take her to other places, even when she doesn't have time for a vacation. Dana lives with her family in Burlington, Connecticut. To learn more about her books, please visit *www.danameachenrau.com*.